Little Acres

David Feela

Little Acres

David Feela

Unsolicited Press
First Edition: August 2018
Copyright© 2018 David Feela
All Rights Reserved
Published by Unsolicited Press

No part of this book may be reproduced or transmitted in any form or by any means without written permission from the publisher or author.

Printed in the United States of America.

Attention schools and businesses: for discounted copies on large orders, please contact the publisher directly.

ISBN: 978-1-947021-87-7

For farmer Pam

GMO free, homegrown: dirt, cows, birds, trees, and a few flowers, mixed with rain and snow, composted and reconstituted as poems.

Contents

Preheat	3
An Inch of Rain	4
How Many Lives Rush Through	5
Etiquette	6
Just the Feeling	7
This Day	8
If Not Now	9
Witching	11
The Shadow the Barn Casts	12
Expecting Rain	13
Hiatus	14
Blue Genes	15
The Wounded Farm	16
Nocturne	17
Still Life	18
Evening Falls	19
Look at the Field	20
Digging a Grave	21
When the Rain Came	22
What the Fields Giveth, the Cows Taketh Away	23
Goethe's Storm Glass	24
Fathoming Sleep	25
In Praise of Insulation	26
Remembering Where We Live	27
As the Cold Becomes You	28

Amaryllis	29
Acknowledgments	30
About the Author	31
About the Press	32

Preheat

Daffodil burns like
a votive beside the sidewalk,
forsythia gushes

like an old gold faithful,
and this incandescent
flame of feather,

bluebird on a wire,
flickers like
the pilot light of spring.

An Inch of Rain

It doesn't sound like much,
being of so little consequence
it barely covers two knuckles
but when you realize
rain comes down like a sheet of plastic
an inch thick, across miles
of undulating farmland, conforming
to its topography,
saturating the trees, leaves
and limbs, clinging to the surface
of lakes for an instant
before being sucked down
into the convection of water tables
and aquifers, then a mere inch
swells to such proportions
it forces the mind to the surface
of simple thought like an ocean buoy,
marking the way to safety.

How Many Lives Rush Through

The mullioned window
makes a pattern on the wall
projected by the evening sun.
I'm counting diamonds,

a jeweler of the ethereal trade
squandering the moment.
In the chair beside me
you read a book, a whodunit

that takes place in Egypt
when pharaohs wore cones of wax
to keep their scalps cooled.
Someone has died, someone

is dying, someone contemplates
death. You pause, looking up
as the desert buries its pyramids
and all my riches fade.

Etiquette

Eagle sits
on his perch, not grand
as an aerie but more
like a porch

at the top of a dead cottonwood,
surveying the field below.
Cows ruminating
on patches of brown,

dog
chasing its tail.
Foolish man
sweeping mud.

Eagle sits,
his circle of light
like water
ripples,

the white head
swivels, yellow beak
like a crooked finger –
Come to me

or wait,
I'll come to you.

Just the Feeling

We wake one morning thinking
just another day, but satellites
colliding in space spread debris

like a shattered glass from last night's
toast to everyone's health,

or the rose blossoming
in a dream field of snow,
a beauty that doesn't belong.

Now you know.
And it's not that you know anything

specific, just that feeling in your gut
urging you awake, whispering
how something isn't right

as sunlight paints the room
a perfect yellow.

This Day

And not any other,
especially not any future day
leaning over the horizon

like a hang glider about to lift off.
This day of imperfect plans,
of decisions to be made

out of habit, of moments
staring into the pantry
and noticing what's in short supply

or what's already been forgotten.
A stockpile and a promise
to be ready, brushing cobwebs

from the ceiling fan,
drinking an extra glass of water.
This long reach into the closet

to bring a sweater forward,
to open a drawer and push a pillow case
back into its nest of dreams.

If Not Now

All of us wait for a particular day,
and that day comes
then goes, to be replaced
by another day

we persistently wait for.
It could be an appointment,
a surgery, a date with a friend
or a lawyer.

It could be a birthday, a picnic,
time for release
from a confinement
where we have been delayed.

It could be a vacation, a flight,
a tour or a performance.
Even a long hallway
with a door that finally shuts.

But it was never
now, never
the inertia required
of a chair,

never the clock irrelevant,
or the water heater's
blue flame maintaining
its temperature.

Never the yard light
burning all night
over the field
where nothing happens.

Witching

The process of searching for and locating
the lost, holding a twig
that dips and twitches as it points

to its mysterious pleasure.
And I'll admit, I've tried.
Picked up a forked stick,

moved slowly about the yard,
but all I found was the root of a tree
where the stick probably came from.

I suspected if I kept it up
I'd find my own grave
so I threw the stick into the bushes

and went about my life in the usual way,
misplacing things and finding them again
when I least expected.

The Shadow the Barn Casts

Early sun makes my barn
grow larger, its shadow stretching
out to the road where traffic

on its way to work
crashes into one side and then
out the other. The chickens squawk,

dust and feathers rising like a storm
against the horizon.
In an hour my barn has shrunk

back into the yard
like the shadow of a hawk
having lit on a power pole,

its appetite sated,
the whole day
devoted to digestion.

Expecting Rain

By daybreak, I'd heard.
Was told.
Believed.
By lunch
clouds pillowed
against clouds
like petals on a gray rose.
I could smell
the aroma of earth
melded to sky,
a vision of virga
floated past.
By six o'clock dust
kicked up in the road
by a stiff wind
moved across the field,
against the horizon.
The air turned yellow
like smoke, igniting
such a glorious sunset
I thought no rain
was worth it.
By bedtime I'd taken my vows,
to believe in nothing
except disappointment
and all the beauty it can bring.

Hiatus

A pot of tea steeps
on the marble sill, steam
clouding the window.

Sunrise on the counter
like the yolk of a broken egg,
Oh! Happy disaster of morning.

All is settled then, the man
still asleep, the woman
keeping time for herself

beside the sink, thinking of every
beginning and ending she's known
before filling her cup.

Blue Genes

He had the brain of a tumbleweed,
the tenacity of a thorn,
the ferocity of a gust
spitting dust across a vacant lot.

She pinned her hopes
to the nearest clothesline,
emptied her heart's basket
before turning back to the house.

Their child stood near the stoop,
gouging the dirt with a stick,
one foot on either side
of a line that grows wider.

The Wounded Farm

From the road nobody can tell who's home.
It looks like a house, a barn, the rusted
remains of a tractor parked
under a cottonwood tree.

The house sits in disrepair, as if the family
had all it could handle
turning earth into cash.
They packed up and headed south

according to neighbors,
and the farm still belongs to
the old man living on the ridge.
Nobody else will rent it.

Nobody wants to tame the urge
to have what they want right now.
Eventually the farm will be plowed under
like the fields around it,

and those blood red sunsets on the ridge,
right where the old farm waits
simply echo the ache
of its hundred little acres.

Nocturne

When it rained last night
I slept through it,
unconscious of the drops
hitting the tin roof
rolling off the eaves.

I dreamt
about places not in the rain,
about cloakrooms and landings
where galoshes wait beside a door.
I must have been tuned to the effort
of trees expanding from inside
one ring at a time.

I wish I'd come awake
just to say to you
who lay sleepless in the dark beside me,
Listen, it's raining!
and all you'd ever have to say back to me is,
I know.

Still Life

As the Great Blue Heron lands
every small thing
turns perfectly still.
Its great blue shadow
sends shivers across the pond.
It wades to the depth
of its spindly legs
then transforms itself
into silence.
Wings tucked,
neck extended,
narrow head with a yellow beak.
As the sun tilts,
in the silt a small thing blinks.

Evening Falls

I could say fall evenings
which would explain why the morning's
so cool, but the kind of fall I mean

rushes over the horizon
even as the sun draws away,
a dark spray that cools the grass,

sends a shimmering vapor
of stars into the sky above it.
It's like a Niagara Falls

as wide as the earth
emptying the universe
into our backyards.

Evening falls
and babies sleep,
the night rushes to fill every gap,

even the hand in the lap
that falls open, five swirling eddies
surfacing in the moonlight.

Look at the Field

It's dirt, or rather
rocks worn into sediment
and everything else you see

erupts from the pleasure
of pressing against it,
epoxy that holds us tight

to the planet, elixir
that mixes with water
and vents green,

more perfect than gold.
Look at the willows
globed by their canopied leaves,

the cattails poking like pillars
up from the bar ditch
where red-winged blackbirds

perch above their cupped nests.
Just look. It's dirt in the mortar,
dirt in the craw,

dirt rising as dust from behind
a plow to burnish
an ordinary sunset.

Digging a Grave

My foot presses the shovel's blade
into the dirt – steel returning
to the earth. The morning feels cool
so the digging warms me
like the sun drawing me
into its pleasure, but this is work.

A grave shakes enthusiasm
and lays it flat. Stones must be
pried loose, tossed onto a pile
that grinds like a mouth full of teeth.
The deeper I go, the softer the soil
as if life's argument against death
had given up its resistance.

I cut the edges straight,
scoop loose dirt from the bottom that fell,
then strike again with the pickaxe,
a little more, and more again,
the spade forever returning
to shape this emptiness.

When the Rain Came

Nothing else mattered. We stopped staring
into that tunnel carved out of plastic and glass,
put the remote down on the little table
where it gathers its warmth from our hands.

Rain hit the roof with more crackle than static,
fell thicker than pixels or peacock tails.
Tree limbs bent like so many antennas
twisting to line up with the wind.

We both stood and faced the picture
window where the landscape muted from green
to gray, the light driven out of the sky
by so much water penetrating its space.

Nothing could have been
more compelling, not the moon breaking
loose like a shock of rigging,
not the flotsam of sodden stars.

What the Fields Giveth, the Cows Taketh Away

Cows concentrate
with their heads down
on what the field preaches –

sunlight warming their hides,
a scent of alfalfa hay,
fresh water in the mud hole
from yesterday's rain.
Any news that rises
ruminates for the day
and faithfully each cow
broadens with praise.

Goethe's Storm Glass

The barometer knows
about change,
pressure fluctuating

like a foot
against the accelerator,
but the animals

also know
and the arthritic bubble
in the old farmer's elbow

and the trees
with their leaves astir
as if to whisper

the weather
from the bottom
of the earth's teacup.

Fathoming Sleep

A down comforter,
feather pillows, flannel sheets,
the soft belly of the bed
exposed so she'll see
no danger.

A robe cascades from her shoulders,
pools on the floor
as she steps into the slipstream.
So fluid the motion
surfaces warm to her skin,

yet she's nudged
still deeper, past the ordinary
dream fish, the coral
clock on a shelf
keeping prehistoric time.

She touches more lives
than a raindrop
summoned through a canopy
of leaves
by the tiniest seed.

In Praise of Insulation

The roof, shed of its snowpack,
gathers the sun's heat again.

Upstairs under the shingles
the attic warms while

outside the temperature
hasn't climbed above freezing.

On such a day I could lift
from the mausoleum of dusty boxes

my dimmest memories and hold them
under the glare of a bare bulb

but it has all been so neatly packed away.
To open one box would only

lead to another, and what is the past
if not an accumulation of things we

cannot touch wrapped up in the feeling
that we also cannot let them go.

Remembering Where We Live

I return to this house so often
I forget it's not where I live,
just where I sleep
with the lights turned off.

I sweep new snow off the porch
but remember it falling
so thick in the woods
the bare trees shivered white.

Animal tracks like a dotted a line
disappear into the bushes
and I remember seeking shelter
in the company of living things

so different from me
all I could do was sit quietly.
From the deep pocket of this moment
I broadcast a handful of stars

that settle into their predictable niches.
Old friends, old light.

As the Cold Becomes You

Imagine below zero
behind your skin, ice
etching lace on your smooth
white teeth, blood turning to slush,
arteries pulsing like blue neon tubes
so that no one walking past
can help but stare at the stillness
you carry inside.
The second hand on your wrist
sweeps the watch crystal clear
so the shadow of a miniature angel
hovers in front of your face.
Three sharp jabs a few decibels
higher than a dog whistle
and all the warning you need
tingles at your extremities.
Go deeper, you think, quickly now,
toward a flicker of warmth,
into that narrow hallway
where a bright door swings open.

Amaryllis

Snow drifts against the picket fence,
icicles won't leave the eaves,
but the amaryllis shows up
in a cardboard box from Virginia
as if riding in its own suitcase,
soil spilling onto the porch
even before the carton can be opened.
It wants to get started.
It requires a south-facing window.
It asks for a drink.
Everything about amaryllis
feels pink, like lingerie
in a basket, painted fingernails,
glossy magazines.
I blush to think
what blossoms it will bring.

Acknowledgments

Some of these poems first appeared in the following journals, occasionally in a slightly different version.

The author gratefully acknowledges both editors and staffs.

Caesura
Kansas City Voices
Labletter
Leaping Clear
Mountain Gazette
New Verse News
Pilgrimage
Ruminate
Southwest Edible
Small Farmer's Journal

About the Author

David Feela, retired from a 27 year teaching career, works as a poet, freelance columnist, and thrift store book collector. He earned an MFA from Vermont College, with undergraduate degrees from St. Cloud State University. His writing has appeared in hundreds of regional and national publications, including syndication by the *High Country News* "Writers on the Range," and *The Denver Post*. Writing has appeared in *Mountain Gazette, Small Farmer's Journal, Utne Reader, the Santa Fe Literary Review*, to name a few. For 11 years Feela served as a contributing editor for the former *Inside/Outside Southwest* magazine. He currently writes monthly columns for the *Four Corners Free Press* and the *Durango Telegraph*.

Feela has authored one poetry chapbook, Thought Experiments (Maverick Press, 1998), winner of the Southwest Poet Series, a full-length poetry edition, *The Home Atlas* (WordTech, 2009), and a collection of essays, *How Delicate These Arches* (Raven's Eye Press, 2012) which was chosen as a creative non-fiction finalist for the Colorado Book Award. A selection of his poetry is forthcoming in volume 2, *The Geography of Hope: Poets of Colorado's Western Slope*, through Conundrum Press. He resides in Cortez, Colorado.

About the Press

Unsolicited Press was founded in 2012. Based in Portland, Oregon, the team seeks to publish fantastic poetry, fiction, and creative nonfiction.

Learn more at www.unsolicitedpress.com

www.ingramcontent.com/pod-product-compliance
Lightning Source LLC
Chambersburg PA
CBHW030135100526
44591CB00009B/676